IMAGES OF CHRISTIANS

8 STUDIES FOR INDIVIDUALS OR GROUPS

LifeGuide®
BIBLE STUDIES

BILL WEIMER

IVP
An imprint of InterVarsity Press
Downers Grove, Illinois

InterVarsity Press
P.O. Box 1400, Downers Grove, IL 60515-1426
ivpress.com
email@ivpress.com

InterVarsity Press® is the book-publishing division of InterVarsity Christian Fellowship/USA®, a movement of students and faculty active on campus at hundreds of universities, colleges, and schools of nursing in the United States of America, and a member movement of the International Fellowship of Evangelical Students. For information about local and regional activities, visit intervarsity.org.

LifeGuide® is a registered trademark of InterVarsity Christian Fellowship.

Cover design: Cindy Kiple
Interior design: Jeanna Wiggins
Cover image: sugar in a bowl: © Suwannar Kawila / EyeEm / Getty Images

ISBN 978-0-8308-3118-0 (print)
ISBN 978-0-8308-6439-3 (digital)

Printed in the United States of America ♾

InterVarsity Press is committed to ecological stewardship and to the conservation of natural resources in all our operations. This book was printed using sustainably sourced paper.

P 25 24 23 22 21 20 19 18 17 16 15 14 13 12 11 10 9 8 7 6 5 4 3 2
Y 36 35 34 33 32 31 30 29 28 27 26 25 24 23 22

CONTENTS

GETTING THE MOST OUT OF *IMAGES OF CHRISTIANS*

We all have images: self-images and others' images of us. Our self-image may or may not be realistic. However, who others imagine us to be sometimes shapes our self-image. Often, others' images of us can be more accurate since such perspectives are based on observations of our behaviors and beliefs.

Images of Christians vary widely:

- Some think Jesus-followers are narrow, prejudiced, nonthinking, hypocritical, stuck-up, judgmental, isolated, unfriendly, selfish, uncaring, and self-centered.
- Others may describe believers as gracious, faithful, kind, sensitive, helpful, insightful, grateful, giving, servants, witnesses, helpers, and other-oriented.

Centuries ago in the Roman Empire, Christians were often inaccurately described in images and terms because their beliefs and behaviors were misunderstood and misinterpreted. They were depicted as

- cannibals: they consumed the Lord's body and blood during Communion.
- incestuous: they related in love to other Christians as sisters and brothers.
- incendiaries: they believed and said the world's political order would soon end in a fiery climax.
- atheists: they did not worship the Roman or Greek gods.
- revolutionaries: their loyalty was not to Caesar or Rome but only to Christ and his kingdom.

Regarding images of early Christians, University of Virginia history professor Robert Wilken notes, "One critic has hinted that the reason

Christianity succeeded in making its way within the Roman world was due less to what Christians believed, than to the way they lived."* *The Epistle to Diognetus*, a second-century document by an unknown author possibly written for a Roman leader, gives us this picture of how Christians lived:

> They love all, and yet are persecuted by all. They are unknown and condemned; they are put to death, yet restored to life. They are poor, yet make many rich; they are in lack of all things, yet abound in all. They are dishonored, yet in their very dishonor are glorified. They are evil spoken of, yet are justified; they are reviled, and bless. They are insulted, yet repay the insult with honor. They do good, yet are punished as evildoers. When punished, they rejoice as if quickened into life. They are assailed by the Jews as foreigners and are persecuted by the Greeks, yet those who hate them are unable to assign any reason for their hatred.**

More importantly, the Bible gives various metaphors and motifs, descriptions and analogies of God's people: a vineyard, dry bones resuscitated, sheep, salt and light, branches, and the body and bride of Christ. Yet less-known images of Christians are also important for us in our image-conscious culture as we seek biblical patterns for our lives. *Images of Christians* examines many of these images and encourages us to grow in grace as we seek to be conformed to the image of Christ.

SUGGESTIONS FOR INDIVIDUAL STUDY

1. As you begin each study, pray that God will speak to you through his Word.

2. Read the introduction to the study and respond to the personal reflection question or exercise. This is designed to help you focus on God and on the theme of the study.

3. Each study deals with a particular passage—so that you can delve into the author's meaning in that context. Read and reread the passage to be studied. If you are studying a book, it will be helpful to read through the entire book prior to the first study. The questions are written using the language of the New International Version, so you may wish to use that version of the Bible. The New Revised Standard Version is also recommended.

4. This is an inductive Bible study, designed to help you discover for yourself what Scripture is saying. The study includes three types of questions. *Observation* questions ask about the basic facts: who, what, when, where, and how. *Interpretation* questions delve into the meaning of the passage. *Application* questions help you discover the implications of the text for growing in Christ. These three keys unlock the treasures of Scripture.

Write your answers to the questions in the spaces provided or in a personal journal. Writing can bring clarity and deeper understanding of yourself and of God's Word.

5. It might be good to have a Bible dictionary handy. Use it to look up any unfamiliar words, names, or places.

6. Use the prayer suggestion to guide you in thanking God for what you have learned and to pray about the applications that have come to mind.

7. You may want to go on to the suggestion under "Now or Later," or you may want to use that idea for your next study.

SUGGESTIONS FOR MEMBERS OF A GROUP STUDY

1. Come to the study prepared. Follow the suggestions for individual study mentioned above. You will find that careful preparation will greatly enrich your time spent in group discussion.

2. Be willing to participate in the discussion. The leader of your group will not be lecturing. Instead, he or she will be encouraging the members of the group to discuss what they have learned. The leader will be asking the questions that are found in this guide.

3. Stick to the topic being discussed. Your answers should be based on the verses which are the focus of the discussion and not on outside authorities such as commentaries or speakers. These studies focus on a particular passage of Scripture. Only rarely should you refer to other portions of the Bible. This allows for everyone to participate in in-depth study on equal ground.

4. Be sensitive to the other members of the group. Listen attentively when they describe what they have learned. You may be surprised by their insights! Each question assumes a variety of answers. Many questions do not have "right" answers, particularly questions that aim at meaning or application. Instead the questions push us to explore the passage more thoroughly.

When possible, link what you say to the comments of others. Also, be affirming whenever you can. This will encourage some of the more hesitant members of the group to participate.

5. Be careful not to dominate the discussion. We are sometimes so eager to express our thoughts that we leave too little opportunity for others to respond. By all means participate! But allow others to also.

6. Expect God to teach you through the passage being discussed and through the other members of the group. Pray that you will have an enjoyable and profitable time together, but also that as a result of the study you will find ways that you can take action individually and/or as a group.

7. Remember that anything said in the group is considered confidential and should not be discussed outside the group unless specific permission is given to do so.

8. If you are the group leader, you will find additional suggestions at the back of the guide.

---

*Robert Louis Wilken, *The Christians as the Romans Saw Them* (New Haven, CT: Yale University Press, 2003), 198.

**"The Manners of Christians," in *The Epistle of Mathetes to Diognetus*, trans. Alexander Roberts and James Donaldson, *Early Christian Writings*, accessed November 19, 2018, www.earlychristianwritings.com/text/diognetus-roberts.html.

ONE

DISCIPLES

Mark 8:27-38

As a young Irish girl Amy Carmichael (1867–1951) invited Christ into her heart. When she was eighteen, because of her devotion to Christ, she invited neighborhood children into her home, educating them and ending each lesson with a gospel song and Bible story. With her strong faith and gracious demeanor, she brought in poor children that most citizens ignored.

When Amy was twenty-six, she departed Ireland as a missionary to Japan. Two years later she went to India, where she founded the Dohnavur Fellowship as a home for young girls fleeing Hindu temple prostitution.

During the last twenty years of her life, Amy was bedridden after severe injuries from a fall. Yet she continued ministering and wrote poetry and thirty-five books about serving Jesus and others with his love. She left her family and homeland to serve Christ for fifty-five years without furlough. At eighty-three Amy Carmichael, a disciple of Christ, died in India.

Group Discussion. In practical terms, what does it mean to be a disciple of another person?

Personal Reflection. If you were to record all of your free-time activities, what would this tell you about who or what you are a disciple of?

Most people in our Western culture know something about Jesus. Yet knowing *about* a person is not the same thing as *knowing* that person. Jesus' question to us and our response to him create the pivotal point in our life—whether we will believe in him, follow him, and become his disciple. *Read Mark 8:27-38.*

1. What two questions does Jesus ask of his disciples (vv. 27, 29)?

2. In our culture, what do people tend to say about Jesus Christ?

3. What is your response to Jesus' question, "Who do you say I am?"

4. If disciples are to spread the good news about Jesus, why do you think he told them not to tell anyone about him (v. 30)?

5. In verse 31, what does Jesus discuss with his disciples?

6. Why might this be linked to his words not to talk about him (v. 30)?

7. How does Peter react to Jesus' predictions (v. 32)?

8. Why do you think Peter responded this way?

9. Why does Jesus rebuke Peter and his questioning?

10. What three things does Jesus say a person must do to be his disciple (v. 34)?

11. Do you think Jesus' teaching in verses 34-38 is too harsh? Why or why not?

12. How have Jesus' words in this study stretched and deepened your image of being a disciple of Christ?

Lord Jesus, you know people hold different views about you. But I believe and confess that you are the Son of God, the Messiah. Teach me how to be your faithful follower and fruitful disciple.

NOW OR LATER

Read John 15:1-8, about being Jesus' disciple.

Take time to read the lyrics of or sing these Amy Carmichael hymns and songs:

"To Calv'ry Let Our Eyes Be Turned"
"O God of Burning Altar Fire"
"Make Me Thy Fuel"
"For Sunrise Hope and Sunset Calm"

TWO

BELOVED FRIENDS

3 John 1:1-14

Two extremely bright and exceptionally creative professors could have been competitive rivals, yet a close friendship and mutual support developed. The faith of the first man, a strong Catholic, slowly seeped into the analytical mind of the second man, who was an atheist. In friendly dialogue they discussed literary myths, religious concepts, and the latter's skepticism.

The second man finally admitted to belief in God in 1929. Two years later he accepted Jesus Christ as the incarnate Son of God. For over two decades these two men, along with several others, met weekly in a college professor's room and in a local pub. They discussed myths and theology, shared creative ideas, and critiqued each other's writings. The unique friendship of J. R. R. Tolkien (1892–1973) and C. S. Lewis (1898–1963) bore much fruit.

Without the professional and personal interaction of Tolkien and Lewis, the world today would not enjoy their creative and widely popular fantasies and nonfiction classics, such as *The Lord of the Rings*, The Chronicles of Narnia series, and *Mere Christianity*. Millions have been stimulated intellectually and strengthened spiritually by their professional and personal friendship.

Group Discussion. What are the fruits of close friendships?

Personal Reflection. Name some beloved friends not near you. How did your friendship deepen and how do you encourage them now?

Along with John's Gospel and Revelation, the three letters 1–3 John are usually attributed to the apostle John, although each of these writings have their own unique literary elements. The epistle of this study, 3 John, is a heartfelt communiqué between two believers. *Read 3 John 1:1-14.*

1. From what you can gather in this letter about their character, describe John and Gaius.

2. John repeatedly addresses Gaius as his "dear friend." What does this tell us about their relationship?

3. Identify a couple of your beloved friends. How do they influence your spiritual life?

4. What are the characteristics of Gaius and the Christians around him that give John "great joy" (vv. 3-4)?

5. What Christians you have worked with, helped, taught, or discipled have given you great joy? Why?

6. What hospitality (vv. 5-8) was being given, by and to whom, and why was this so important?

7. In our culture, is hospitality vital among and by Christians? How and why?

8. Describe what John identifies as a congregational problem where Gaius is (vv. 9-10)?

9. Why did Diotrephes act as he did with visitors?

10. Who are three or four believers you have welcomed into your fellowship?

How did you do this?

What further ways might you deepen and develop your friendship?

Lord, enable me to welcome, befriend, and assimilate into your church those who are new disciples of Jesus. May I never exclude, ignore, or avoid such believers, even seekers, coming to our group, fellowship, or congregation. May I not only assist them but also learn from them.

NOW OR LATER

Study John 15:9-17 to learn more about true friendship with Jesus and others.

THREE

GIVERS

2 Corinthians 8:1-15; 9:6-15

Born into British nobility in 1707, Selina Hastings later married the 9th Earl of Huntingdon in 1728. After the 1746 death of her husband, she became a supporter of preachers and evangelists John Wesley and George Whitefield during the eighteenth-century evangelical spiritual revival. To assist this revival she established and funded sixty-four chapels in England and oversaw the appointment of like-minded clergy for each. In 1768 she founded a ministers' training college, incorporated later into the University of Cambridge. She also funded missionaries to New Brunswick and Nova Scotia. Over her lifetime, she gave between $250,000 and $300,000 to support Christian causes.

In her will Selina requested that no biography be written about her. None were until ninety years after her death. She was described as "the patriarchess of the Methodists" and a vital donor of the Evangelical Revival in England. Fifty years after she died, Cardinal John Henry Newman praised her: "She devoted herself, her name, her means, her time, and her thoughts, to the cause of Christ. She did not spend her money on herself. She did not allow the homage paid to her rank to remain with herself."*

Through her family influence, personal initiatives, and financial assets, no one was a more generous giver to various Christian causes in the eighteenth century than Selina, Countess of Huntingdon (1707–1791).

Group Discussion. When people are pressured to give money, what are various individual responses?

Personal Reflection. What are your personal feelings about giving money? Who or what do you fund and why?

This study includes a long passage of Scripture, but it is critical to understanding financial support of Christian groups and ministries. The people of Jerusalem and Judea periodically suffered famines during Emperor Claudius's reign (AD 41–54). As the apostle Paul maintained continuous contact with congregations in those areas, he was concerned with their condition, spiritually and economically. So, when he visited the Macedonian and Greek churches, Paul solicited financial aid to send to the Christians in Jerusalem and Judea. He writes that generosity in giving is both an issue of food and of faith, economics and spirituality. *Read 2 Corinthians 8:1-15.*

1. What has occurred in the Macedonian churches, and how does Paul commend these churches?

2. Paul says the Macedonian churches "gave as much as they were able" and "pleaded . . . for the privilege of sharing" with other Christians (vv. 3-4). Is this the attitude of most Western Christians today? Why or why not?

3. Giving by Macedonian believers exceeded Paul's expectations. What kind of financial giving do you think is expected of Christians today (v. 5)?

4. How does Paul reason from the Corinthians' self-image (v. 7) and why?

5. In verses 10-13, how does Paul explain giving and receiving?

6. Paul says the goal in giving and receiving is "equality" (vv. 13-14). How does he explain what he means by this?

7. *Read 2 Corinthians 9:6-15.* Paul argues that those who give sparingly reap sparingly, and those who give generously reap generously. When have you given sparingly or generously? What were the results?

8. Paul uses the imagery of seed, sower, and harvest (vv. 10-11). How have you seen this teaching apply to your life?

9. How does Paul link our Christian confession (v. 13) with our giving, our belief with our behavior? Do you agree?

10. Review your giving attitudes and actions. If you are willing, tell the group how this Scripture challenges or confirms what you give.

O God, remind me that all I have are gifts from you. Help me to honor and glorify you by assisting Christian ministries and others in Christ's name. Grant me wisdom not to hoard my money but rather to use it generously for you and others.

NOW OR LATER

Next time you are about to support Christian or charitable groups, (1) pray for them, their staff, and people they serve, and then (2) write your checks or transmit your funds.

For a more thorough understanding of New Testament teaching on money and giving, study the following passages: Mark 10:17-23; 12:41-44; Luke 6:38; 19:1-10; Acts 4:32-35; 5:1-11; 2 Corinthians 12:11-15.

*John Henry Newman, *The Works of Cardinal Newman*, vol. 1 (London: Longmans, Green, and Co., 1897), 388.

FOUR

AMBASSADORS

2 Corinthians 5:14-21

During the Fifth Crusade (1217–1221), crusaders fought Muslims in the Holy Land and in Egypt. In 1219, with indecisive soldiers' battles and little spiritual impact in the region, a strong but simple Christian leader felt compelled to take the gospel to the region.

Francis of Assisi went to Damietta, Egypt, where crusaders and Muslims struggled in close quarters for the Muslim headquarters. Francis allowed himself and a Franciscan brother to be captured and dragged before the powerful Muslim sultan Malik al-Kamil. The sultan was tired of the fighting and wondered if this diminutive, barefoot man brought a peace treaty. The sultan questioned the captive monk dressed in simple peasant's clothes: Who did he represent and why had he come?

Later records tell of their dialogue. Francis courageously explained that he was sent by God, not by men—knowing he might be martyred for his Christian faith. He explained the triune God and that Jesus Christ is the messenger and mediator of love, forgiveness, and reconciliation between God and all people. When asked if they represented the pope and his crusader army, Francis replied that he was not the pope's emissary—"We are ambassadors for the Lord Jesus Christ."

The sultan was impressed not only with Francis's clear convictions but also his humble demeanor, encouraging the gracious monk to stay a while. The Muslim leader offered valuable gifts to Francis, who respectfully refused them, thereby enhancing the sultan's respect for this Christian. Preparing for Francis to be escorted safely back to the Christians' camp, the sultan requested, "Pray to God for me, that God might reveal to me the law and faith more pleasing to him." With gentleness and respect, Francis was an exemplary ambassador for Christ.*

Group Discussion. What are the responsibilities of a political ambassador? What image do ambassadors have in the nations they are assigned to?

Personal Reflection. If you were an ambassador to a hostile or indifferent nation, what means of communication would best express goodwill to that nation?

The Corinthian people lived in a rather sophisticated, intellectual, and elitist society. So when some citizens became followers of Jesus, they struggled with and even slipped back into their past mindsets. As an ambassador of Christ, Paul struggled to persuade others and remind Corinthian Christians of the good news of Christ's death and resurrection to new life. *Read 2 Corinthians 5:14-21.*

1. As an ambassador of Christ, what is Paul compelled to communicate and why (vv. 14-15)?

2. What does it mean to regard someone from a "worldly point of view" (v. 16)?

How has Paul's perspective changed?

3. What is the good news "in Christ" (v. 17)?

How would you describe changes that occur in a new Christian?

4. If you are comfortable doing so, explain what has changed in you since you began to earnestly follow Christ.

5. Paul says we are reconciled to God through Christ. What was our prior status with God (vv. 18-19)?

6. As Christ's ambassadors, what is our message to others on behalf of God (vv. 19-20)?

7. Verse 20 includes two sentences. In the second sentence do you think Paul is imploring Christians to be reconciled to God? Or is he stating what Christ's ambassadors' (Christians) message is to those who are not currently following Christ?

8. Review this passage. What most motivates you to be a witness on behalf of Christ?

9. This week, who will you be an ambassador to with the gospel?

O Lord, thank you for sending Jesus to reveal your merciful character, to reconcile us to you through his death and resurrection, and to teach us about your magnificent kingdom. Make me a faithful ambassador of Jesus Christ that I might share and show his good news to those around me. Amen.

NOW OR LATER

Read these passages about "envoys-ambassadors" for principles in your witness to your culture:

Biblical Passages	Observations and Interpretation	Applications Possible for an Ambassador for Christ
Numbers 20:14-17 Joshua 9:3-6 2 Samuel 8:9-10 1 Kings 5:1 2 Chronicles 35:21 Ezekiel 17:12-15		

*Paul Moses, "Men of Peace: What We Can Learn from St. Francis & the Sultan," *Commonweal*, October 3, 2019, www.commonwealmagazine.org/men-peace; and Navid Zaidi, "St. Francis of Assisi and Sultan al-Kamil: A Bold Christian-Muslim Encounter," *Sufi Ways* (blog), May 2, 2016, https://sufiways.com/2016/05/02/st-francis-of-assisi-and-sultan-al-kamil.

FIVE

RESCUEES

Colossians 1:9-14, 21-23

Being lost in darkness can cause fear and death. In 2018 the world prayed for twelve boys trapped with their soccer coach in an underground Thailand cave as rising floodwaters threatened them. In 2010 the world prayed for thirty-three miners in a collapsed Chilean cave, a half-mile underground and three miles from the blocked exit. These boys and miners, after seventeen days and sixty-nine days respectively, were miraculously rescued. But more deadly is being trapped in spiritual darkness—and not knowing it!

In the 1950s and 1960s Rev. David Wilkerson (1931–2011) was an evangelist and pastor to gang members and drug users in New York City. He befriended them patiently and shared God's grace persistently. Through him and the Holy Spirit, some were rescued out of the darkness and into the kingdom of light.

New York gang leader and drug dealer Nicky Cruz, a young man whose Puerto Rican parents were spiritualists, was converted to Jesus Christ and changed into a new person. Wilkerson's book about this spiritual rescue, *The Cross and the Switchblade*, sold over fifteen million copies. Later Cruz, who tells his story in *Run Baby Run*, led teen ministries in New York and California and held evangelistic meetings overseas. He was rescued from dominions of darkness and brought into the kingdom of God's light and love.

Group Discussion. Imagine you have been trapped in a dark, dank cave for sixty-nine days. What emotions would you experience when you were rescued and brought into the light and fresh air and warmth and love?

Personal Reflection. Have you been transferred from spiritual darkness into Christ's light? If so, when and how? If not, do you wish to be?

The original readers of Paul's letter to the church in Colossae probably became Christians through Epaphras. Examining the first and fourth chapters of Colossians, we discover he was a Colossian who brought the gospel to this city and apparently to neighboring towns Laodicea and Hierapolis. He is a faithful minister, an intermediary in correspondence and prayer, and a hard worker for these believers. *Read Colossians 1:9-14.*

1. Since Paul first learned about the faith and love of the Colossians, he has asked God for certain things on their behalf. Put in your own words what his prayer for them entails (vv. 9-12).

2. What is the source of the knowledge of God's will (v. 9)?

3. What is the purpose of obtaining wisdom and understanding (v. 10)?

4. Because God has rescued us from the dominion of darkness (v. 13), we can now "live a life worthy of the Lord" (v. 10). In what four ways does this manifest itself (vv. 10-12)?

5. Which of these aspects of the rescued life are you seeking?

6. *Read Colossians 1:21-23.* Prior to being rescued by Christ, what was our status before God?

Now that we are rescued and reconciled to God through Christ's death, what is our status before God?

7. What is the implication of the conditional clause ("if . . .") in verse 23?

8. What is the "hope held out in the gospel" (v. 23)?

9. Because God has rescued you in Christ, what specific measures can you take to increase in one of these ways of walking worthy of the Lord: bearing fruit, growing in the knowledge of God, being strengthened in endurance and patience, and giving joyful thanks to the Father?

Lord, I was in darkness, though I didn't realize it. But you rescued me and brought me into the light and love of your kingdom by Jesus Christ. For the spiritual changes you made and are making in me, I praise you.

NOW OR LATER

Study Isaiah 9:1-7 about who will bring light and peace to those in darkness. Or study 1 Peter 2:4-12 for images and descriptions of how believers are changed by the living Stone.

SIX

RECONCILERS

Philemon 1-25

Corrie and her Christian family hid Jews from Nazis in their Dutch home in the 1940s. After two years their hiding place was discovered. The family was arrested and split apart, and they never saw each other again, except Corrie and an older sister, Betsie, who were imprisoned together. After ten months Betsie died in the concentration camp. The younger sister did not die but was released by "a clerical error."

Following the war Corrie started an evangelistic ministry. One day a unique confrontation ensued after she spoke in Munich.

> I saw him, working his way forward. One moment, I saw the overcoat and brown hat; the next, a blue uniform and visor cap with its skull and crossbones. It came back with a rush: huge room; harsh overhead lights; pathetic pile of dresses and shoes in the center of the floor; shame of walking naked past this man. . . . The place was Ravensbruck and the man had been one of the cruelest guards.
>
> "You mentioned Ravensbruck in your talk. I was a guard there. But I have become a Christian. I know God has forgiven me for the cruel things I did there, but I would like to hear it from your lips, Fraulein." Again the hand came out, "Will you forgive me?" . . .
>
> "Jesus, help me!" I prayed silently. . . . "I forgive you, brother! With all my heart."*

In Jesus Christ, an evil Nazi concentration camp guard had been reconciled to God and also to a former prisoner, Corrie ten Boom (1892–1983).

Group Discussion. When nations, races, ethnic groups, or political parties hate, is reconciliation possible? How?

Personal Reflection. Has it been hard to forgive someone who wronged you? What were your emotions and thoughts?

This short New Testament letter teaches how becoming a Christian changes relationships with God and with others. In the ancient world many people, including Christians, had slaves of various categories experiencing widely different conditions. Jesus and the apostles, along with their God, expected humane treatment of all people, including slaves. What should be the relationship in Christ between an owner and a slave? The letter to Philemon addressed this dilemma. *Read Philemon 1-25.*

1. What is Paul's current status (v. 1), and who is with him (vv. 23-24)?

Who is the letter written to?

2. What specifically does Paul pray for Philemon (vv. 4-6)?

3. How does Philemon's love refresh Paul and believers (v. 7)?

In what ways can you refresh other Christians?

4. Who is Onesimus, and what broke his relationship with Philemon (vv. 15-16)?

5. Though Onesimus is Philemon's slave, Paul loves Onesimus as a son (v. 10) and brother (v. 16) in Christ. What is Paul asking Philemon to do about Onesimus (vv. 16-17)?

6. What does this letter teach us about how we should relate to those we might consider of lower social, economic, or workplace status than we are?

7. What factors does Paul mention in his appeal to Philemon regarding Onesimus (vv. 17-21)?

8. How will Paul experience restoration with Philemon and Colossian Christians (v. 22)?

9. What practical ways can you be a reconciler among your friends or in your church?

Is there anyone in your life right now that you need to be reconciled to? What can you do to pursue reconciliation with that person?

Lord, I have done things that have broken my relationship with you and with others. For these actions and attitudes, I am sorry. Forgive me through your Son Jesus. May your grace reconcile me to you and to others. Amen.

NOW OR LATER

Young Joseph was separated from his family when his brothers sold him into slavery (Genesis 37). Study Genesis 45:1-11 and 50:15-21 to learn how Joseph became reconciled to his brothers.

Study Luke 15:11-32 about a rebellious son and his reconciliation with his loving father.

---

*Corrie ten Boom, *Tramp for the Lord* in *Corrie Ten Boom: Her Story* (New York: Inspirational Press, 1995), 217-18.

SEVEN

RUNNERS

Hebrews 12:1-13

Eight-year-old Glenn's legs were severely burned in a traumatic schoolhouse fire in Elkhart, Kansas. Doctors recommended amputating his legs, but Glenn was so distressed that his parents would not allow it. The doctors predicted he might never walk, and if he did, he would not walk normally. But through determination and hours of rehab, he started walking, then jogging, and finally running. He had a positive attitude and a strong religious faith, having made a commitment to Jesus Christ as a young boy.

In his twenties, Glenn ran in two Summer Olympics, setting records in the 1,500-meter and mile races. After retiring from running, he and his wife developed a Christian youth ranch named for him in Kansas, where they helped raise and minister to ten thousand needy and abused children.

Glenn Cunningham (1909–1988) was not only a great runner, he also helped young men and women run the race "marked out for us, fixing our eyes on Jesus, the pioneer and perfecter of faith" (Hebrews 12:1-2).

Group Discussion. Describe a time when you were in training. What was the purpose of your practices? What were the results?

Personal Reflection. Did you ever run a race or do a long charity walk? If so, what obstacles or challenges did you face?

The Scriptures periodically use running to illustrate life and spiritual progress in faith (for example, Isaiah 40:28-31; 1 Corinthians 9:24-27). In this study the letter to the Hebrews describes Christians using the imagery of running a race. *Read Hebrews 12:1-13.*

1. What is the overarching theme of this passage of Scripture?

2. If you have run a race (or jogged), what were the challenges you faced and how did you deal with these?

3. What must we "throw off" and why (v. 1)?

4. Why should we "fix our eyes" on Jesus as we run (v. 2)?

5. How did Jesus run his race, respond to his obstacles, and accomplish his goal (v. 2)?

Does his endurance and perseverance motivate you? Explain.

6. Why does the writer bring up "the Lord's discipline" (vv. 5-6)?

How is discipline related to running the race marked out for us?

7. The author suggests that "hardship" is good for us (v. 7). Why?

8. What is the goal of God's discipline, of persevering in a grueling race (vv. 10-11)?

9. Hebrews teaches that the Christian life can be viewed as a race toward a finish line. What is one discipline you will embrace as you "run with perseverance the race marked out for us" (v. 1)?

Lord, as I go through life, things can be difficult. Obstacles and obstructions, hindrances and hurdles impede or trip up my spiritual progress. Grant me perseverance. Bring to mind past Christians examples for me—especially Jesus, who endured and accomplished his race—so I will not grow weary and lose heart. Amen.

NOW OR LATER

Read Isaiah 40:28-31 to learn that God understands how tired and worn out we get, and how he encourages as we run the faith journey of life.

Study 2 Timothy 4:6-8 to see the award we will receive when we have kept the faith and finished the race.

EIGHT

WORSHIPERS

Revelation 5:1-14; 19:1-8

Fanny **became ill** several weeks after her 1820 birth. The family doctor was out of town, so a person claiming to be a physician treated her, placing mustard plasters on her infected eyes, which apparently scarred them—she was blind for life. Months later her father died; her mother had to work to support the family. Her grandmother, a strong Christian, raised her. With her sharp mind, this blind child memorized much Scripture and developed a poetic mind.

Fanny created almost nine thousand hymns, including "To God Be the Glory," "Praise Him! Praise Him! Jesus Our Blessed Redeemer!" and "Blessed Assurance." All her hymns encourage us to worship Jesus.

When we see Jesus described in the New Testament, do we—with the same heart and vision of Fanny Crosby (1820-1915)—worship the Savior? Because of her blindness, she said the first face she would ever see would be in heaven: the risen and reigning Lord Jesus. Her hymn "Give Me Jesus" expresses her "sight" and worship.

Group Discussion. What hymns or choruses best help you to prepare for worship?

Personal Reflection. What is the most meaningful worship experience you have had? What Scriptures inspire you to worship Christ Jesus?

Revelation unveils the pinnacle purpose and power of God in history as Victor and Conqueror over evil. It expresses the ultimate characteristic for Christians: We are not called to be good people or church members, witnesses or Bible study leaders, or Christian leaders or pastors. The people of God are called to worship the Lord! *Read Revelation 5:1-14.*

1. In a vision the apostle John is ushered into the heavenly throne room (see Revelation 4:1-2). The person sitting on the throne holds a scroll in his hand. What is the problem expressed by the mighty angel (Revelation 5:2-3)?

How does John react to this situation?

2. How is John comforted (v. 5)?

3. Who is this "Lion of Judah" (v. 5)?

4. Describe the scene John next sees (vv. 6-10).

Who now is at the center of this scene?

Why is the Lamb worthy of opening the scroll and receiving worship (v. 9)?

5. Identify the four different groups who worship the Lamb (vv. 6-14).

6. What causes you to "fall down" before the Lord in song or in silence, in praise and prayer?

7. *Read Revelation 19:1-8.* Describe the scene as Revelation comes to a climax.

8. As they worship, what do the four living creatures, the twenty-four elders, and the multitudes praise God for?

9. What are a few things you can do to enhance your worship of the Lamb who stands at the center of the throne?

O Lord, quiet me in your presence. Deepen my worship of you—God the Father, Almighty Creator; God the Son, Jesus Christ crucified and risen; and God the Holy Spirit, the breath of spiritual life. I bow before you in worship, through the Lamb of God who was slain for me. Amen.

NOW OR LATER

Study Revelation 1:1-18 and 5:14, then worship anew the Lamb of God, the risen and reigning Lord Jesus Christ.

LEADER'S NOTES

My grace is sufficient for you.

2 CORINTHIANS 12:9

Leading a Bible discussion can be an enjoyable and rewarding experience. But it can also be *scary*—especially if you've never done it before. If this is your feeling, you're in good company. When God asked Moses to lead the Israelites out of Egypt, he replied, "Please send someone else" (Exodus 4:13). It was the same with Solomon, Jeremiah, and Timothy, but God helped these people in spite of their weaknesses, and he will help you as well.

You don't need to be an expert on the Bible or a trained teacher to lead a Bible discussion. The idea behind these inductive studies is that the leader guides group members to discover for themselves what the Bible has to say. This method of learning will allow group members to remember much more of what is said than a lecture would.

These studies are designed to be led easily. As a matter of fact, the flow of questions through the passage from observation to interpretation to application is so natural that you may feel that the studies lead themselves. This study guide is also flexible. You can use it with a variety of groups—student, professional, neighborhood, or church groups. Each study takes forty-five to sixty minutes in a group setting.

There are some important facts to know about group dynamics and encouraging discussion. The suggestions listed below should enable you to effectively and enjoyably fulfill your role as leader.

PREPARING FOR THE STUDY

1. Ask God to help you understand and apply the passage in your own life. Unless this happens, you will not be prepared to lead others. Pray too for the various members of the group. Ask God to open your hearts to the message of his Word and motivate you to action.

2. Read the introduction to the entire guide to get an overview of the entire book and the issues which will be explored.

3. As you begin each study, read and reread the assigned Bible passage to familiarize yourself with it.

4. This study guide is based on the New International Version of the Bible. It will help you and the group if you use this translation as the basis for your study and discussion.

5. Carefully work through each question in the study. Spend time in meditation and reflection as you consider how to respond.

6. Write your thoughts and responses in the space provided in the study guide. This will help you to express your understanding of the passage clearly.

7. It might help to have a Bible dictionary handy. Use it to look up any unfamiliar words, names, or places. (For additional help on how to study a passage, see chapter five of *How to Lead a LifeGuide Bible Study,* InterVarsity Press.)

8. Consider how you can apply the Scripture to your life. Remember that the group will follow your lead in responding to the studies. They will not go any deeper than you do.

9. Once you have finished your own study of the passage, familiarize yourself with the leader's notes for the study you are leading. These are designed to help you in several ways. First, they tell you the purpose the study guide author had in mind when writing the study. Take time to think through how the study questions work together to accomplish that purpose. Second, the notes provide you with additional background information or suggestions on group dynamics for various questions. This information can be useful when people have difficulty understanding or answering a question. Third, the leader's notes can alert you to potential problems you may encounter during the study.

10. If you wish to remind yourself of anything mentioned in the leader's notes, make a note to yourself below that question in the study.

LEADING THE STUDY

1. Begin the study on time. Open with prayer, asking God to help the group to understand and apply the passage.

2. Be sure that everyone in your group has a study guide. Encourage the group to prepare beforehand for each discussion by reading the introduction to the guide and by working through the questions in the study.

3. At the beginning of your first time together, explain that these studies are meant to be discussions, not lectures. Encourage the members of the group to participate. However, do not put pressure on those who may be hesitant to speak during the first few sessions. You may want to suggest the following guidelines to your group.

- Stick to the topic being discussed.
- Your responses should be based on the verses which are the focus of the discussion and not on outside authorities such as commentaries or speakers.
- These studies focus on a particular passage of Scripture. Only rarely should you refer to other portions of the Bible. This allows for everyone to participate in in-depth study on equal ground.
- Anything said in the group is considered confidential and will not be discussed outside the group unless specific permission is given to do so.
- We will listen attentively to each other and provide time for each person present to talk.
- We will pray for each other.

4. Have a group member read the introduction at the beginning of the discussion.

5. Every session begins with a group discussion question. The question or activity is meant to be used before the passage is read. The question introduces the theme of the study and encourages group members to begin to open up. Encourage as many members as possible to participate, and be ready to get the discussion going with your own response.

This section is designed to reveal where our thoughts or feelings need to be transformed by Scripture. That is why it is especially important not to read the passage before the discussion question is asked. The passage will tend to color the honest reactions people would otherwise give because they are, of course, supposed to think the way the Bible does.

You may want to supplement the group discussion question with an icebreaker to help people to get comfortable. See the community section of *Small Group Idea Book* for more ideas.

You also might want to use the personal reflection question with your group. Either allow a time of silence for people to respond individually or discuss it together.

6. Have a group member (or members if the passage is long) read aloud the passage to be studied. Then give people several minutes to read the passage again silently so that they can take it all in.

7. Question 1 will generally be an overview question designed to briefly survey the passage. Encourage the group to look at the whole passage, but try to avoid getting sidetracked by questions or issues that will be addressed later in the study.

8. As you ask the questions, keep in mind that they are designed to be used just as they are written. You may simply read them aloud. Or you may prefer to express them in your own words.

There may be times when it is appropriate to deviate from the study guide. For example, a question may have already been answered. If so, move on to the next question. Or someone may raise an important question not covered in the guide. Take time to discuss it, but try to keep the group from going off on tangents.

9. Avoid answering your own questions. If necessary, repeat or rephrase them until they are clearly understood. Or point out something you read in the leader's notes to clarify the context or meaning. An eager group quickly becomes passive and silent if they think the leader will do most of the talking.

10. Don't be afraid of silence. People may need time to think about the question before formulating their answers.

11. Don't be content with just one answer. Ask, "What do the rest of you think?" or "Anything else?" until several people have given answers to the question.

12. Acknowledge all contributions. Try to be affirming whenever possible. Never reject an answer. If it is clearly off-base, ask, "Which verse led you to that conclusion?" or again, "What do the rest of you think?"

13. Don't expect every answer to be addressed to you, even though this will probably happen at first. As group members become more at ease, they will begin to truly interact with each other. This is one sign of healthy discussion.

14. Don't be afraid of controversy. It can be very stimulating. If you don't resolve an issue completely, don't be frustrated. Move on and keep it in mind for later. A subsequent study may solve the problem.

15. Periodically summarize what the group has said about the passage. This helps to draw together the various ideas mentioned and gives continuity to the study. But don't preach.

16. At the end of the Bible discussion you may want to allow group members a time of quiet to work on an idea under "Now or Later." Then discuss what you experienced. Or you may want to encourage group members to work on these ideas between meetings. Give an opportunity during the session for people to talk about what they are learning.

17. Conclude your time together with conversational prayer, adapting the prayer suggestion at the end of the study to your group. Ask for God's help in following through on the commitments you've made.

18. End on time.

Many more suggestions and helps are found in *How to Lead a LifeGuide Bible Study,* which is part of the LifeGuide Bible Study series.

COMPONENTS OF SMALL GROUPS

A healthy small group should do more than study the Bible. There are four components to consider as you structure your time together.

Nurture. Small groups help us to grow in our knowledge and love of God. Bible study is the key to making this happen and is the foundation of your small group.

Community. Small groups are a great place to develop deep friendships with other Christians. Allow time for informal interaction before and after each study. Plan activities and games that will help you get to know each other. Spend time having fun together—going on a picnic or cooking dinner together.

Worship and prayer. Your study will be enhanced by spending time praising God together in prayer or song. Pray for each other's needs—and keep track of how God is answering prayer in your group. Ask God to help you to apply what you are learning in your study.

Outreach. Reaching out to others can be a practical way of applying what you are learning, and it will keep your group from becoming self-focused. Host a series of evangelistic discussions for your friends or neighbors. Clean up the yard of an elderly friend. Serve at a soup kitchen together, or spend a day working on a Habitat house.

Many more suggestions and helps in each of these areas are found in *Small Group Idea Book.* Information on building a small group can be found in *Small Group Leaders' Handbook* and *The Big Book on Small Groups* (both from InterVarsity Press). Reading through one of these books would be worth your time.

STUDY 1. DISCIPLES. MARK 8:27-38

PURPOSE: To examine what it means to be a follower and disciple of Jesus Christ.

Questions 2-3. It is one thing to know *about* a person but a totally different thing actually to *know* the person. This is the center, the crux, of Mark's Gospel: Who is Jesus and what does it mean to be his disciple? From now on in this Gospel, there will be no more miracles and few crowd engagements. Instead, Jesus will be reinforcing his disciples' understanding of his mission and his method—his crucifixion and his resurrection. It is still good news, but not exactly as his followers had anticipated. Some have called Mark's Gospel the story of the cross with a long introduction.

Question 4. A few scholars called Jesus' instruction here—to keep quiet about him—"the messianic secret." Yet this guidance was only temporary until Jesus could thoroughly explain his pending arrest, trial, and crucifixion. The disciples needed to grasp that the Messiah's method of salvation was not by political, social, or economic revolution. We would be saved through his substitutionary atonement on the cross, through his resurrection over death, and through new spiritual birth in individual lives. After conquering the tomb, Jesus instructed the disciples to go into the world baptizing, teaching, and bearing witness to him (Matthew 28:18-20; Acts 1:4-8). No longer a secret to be kept quiet, now the good news was to be proclaimed far and wide.

Question 9. Jesus rebukes Peter's rebuke because this disciple, like each of us, must have God's perspectives—not our own or that of Satan's, for he is the adversary.

Questions 10-11. Christian discipleship is not a once-and-done decision; it is a daily denial of self and following of Jesus, not a sophisticated, showy status but a humble daily process. The word *disciple* occurs over two hundred times in the New Testament with almost all uses found in the Gospels and Acts. In *Hard Sayings of the Bible*, biblical scholar F. F. Bruce expresses the seriousness of Jesus' challenge about becoming his disciple:

> Jesus' words about the necessity of denying oneself if one wishes to be his disciple . . . is a phrase that has become unconscionably weakened in pious phraseology. Denying oneself is not a matter of giving up something, whether for Lent or for the whole of life; it is a decisive saying no to oneself, to one's hopes and plans and ambitions, to one's likes and dislikes, to one's nearest and dearest, for the sake of Christ. It was so for the first disciples, and it is so for disciples today. But if this is how it is to be taken—and this is how it was meant to be taken—it is a hard saying indeed. (Walter C. Kaiser Jr. et al., *Hard Sayings of the Bible* [Downers Grove, IL: InterVarsity Press, 1996], 428)

STUDY 2. BELOVED FRIENDS. 3 JOHN 1:1-14

PURPOSE: To realize that in Christ and as members of his church we are to be beloved friends with each other, receiving and supporting all believers.

Question 1. John is "the elder," a respected leader to this church. He is close to Gaius ("dear friend") and freely expresses his love toward him. John is vitally concerned about the truth, mentioning it five times. He is hospitable and honors God. Gaius is a faithful Christian, "walking in the truth." He is loving and hospitable, even to strangers.

Question 6. In the ancient Mediterranean culture (and still today), hospitality was a foundational value: to welcome, to feed, and often to house visitors and even travelers. Thus, Christians faithfully extended hospitality to journeying evangelists, teachers, and believers.

Question 9. John hopes to visit this congregation and to address the self-centered, controlling behavior of Diotrephes. The Christian church can never be a limited, closed, secret, or elitist organization; it is a fellowship in and because of Jesus Christ!

STUDY 3. GIVERS. 2 CORINTHIANS 8:1-15; 9:6-15

PURPOSE: To learn from Paul's advice about giving financial support to other Christians and to observe the examples he gives of such generosity.

Question 1. Paul seeks financial aid from one congregation, the Corinthian church, to support needy Christians in other churches. He cites the example of Macedonian Christians (Philippi, Thessalonica, Berea), who, though they faced extreme poverty, gave to others generously, above and beyond the call of duty.

Question 2. Robert Banks and Paul Stevens offer this insight:

> Gift-giving is a thermometer of the soul. . . . Ironically, the very rich are sometimes less generous because their gifts often come with strings attached as a form of control; the very poor, with apparently little to give away, may give their last loaf of bread. . . . Gift-receiving is also a thermometer of the soul . . . [and] usually harder. Sometimes the reluctance or refusal to receive a gift indicates the absolute need for independence and fear of being under obligation to perform some duty in return. Both giving and receiving gifts are not only thermometers of generosity and love; they are also barometers that indicate which way the soul is changing. (Robert Banks and R. Paul Stevens, eds., *The Complete Book of Everyday Christianity* [Downers Grove, IL: InterVarsity Press, 1997], 451-52)

Questions 5-6. This is an opportunity for the Corinthian Christians to assist their less fortunate Judean brothers and sisters. Just as Christ became poor for us (v. 9), we should be willing to share what we have with others. Where there is caring, there will be sharing. Giving does not start with one's wallet or purse, checkbook or financial account! It starts in one's heart, remembering our funds are really God's, loaned to us for our wise and generous stewardship!

Paul did not imply every Corinthian Christian should give the exact same contribution, but according to their means (v. 11). Equality (v. 13) is not the gift amount but rather it is the giving attitude, as Jesus declares in Mark 12:41-44, and reciprocal giving when the need arises (see Jesus' comment in Luke 6:38)

Question 9. How we give and receive gifts reveals a lot about us.

> Gift-giving and receiving begins as it did for the apostle Paul, with giving ourselves to God (2 Cor 8:5). . . . In the end, our giving and receiving tells as much about our spiritually as our prayer life; indeed, they are each a reflection of the other. . . . Giving and receiving are thermometers and barometers of the soul. (Banks and Stevens, *Complete Book of Everyday Christianity*, 455)

STUDY 4. AMBASSADORS. 2 CORINTHIANS 5:14-21

PURPOSE: To understand that we are Christ's messengers and ambassadors taking the good news to others.

Question 2. The worldly point of view is largely transactional; that is, others are viewed in terms of how they can benefit us, what they can do for us to further our emotional, social, or financial status. Christ's followers see people not as objects to be used but as individuals to care for, to want the best for, to love. In his essay "The Weight of Glory," C. S. Lewis observes,

> It is a serious thing to live in a society of possible gods and goddesses, to remember that the dullest and most uninteresting person you talk to may one day be a creature which, if you saw it now, you would be strongly tempted to worship, or else a horror and a corruption such as you now meet, if at all, only in a nightmare. All day long we are, in some degree, helping each other to one or the other of these destinations. It is in the light of these overwhelming possibilities, it is with the awe and the circumspection proper to them, that we should conduct all our dealings with one another, all friendships, all loves, all play, all politics. There are no *ordinary* people. You have never talked to a mere mortal. (C. S. Lewis, *The Weight of Glory* [Grand Rapids, MI: Eerdmans, 1949], 14-15)

Question 3. We have been made new in Christ. We are reconciled to God and ushered into his kingdom. We have been given the Holy Spirit, who empowers us to live a new way. We are no longer slaves to sin. We are free to love God and others, even our enemies.

Question 5. Paul teaches that prior to being reconciled to God, we were ungodly, sinners, spiritually powerless, and even God's enemies (see Romans 5:6-10).

STUDY 5. RESCUEES. COLOSSIANS 1:9-14, 21-23

PURPOSE: To appreciate and appropriate Paul's image of Christians being rescued from the dominion of darkness and relocated into Christ's kingdom of light.

Background. Rescue events and images repeatedly saturate Scriptures.

> The Bible is filled with stories and images of rescue. It is an anthology of rescue stories, spoken and written by people who had themselves participated in a grand rescue and who want their listeners and readers to be recipients of rescue also. . . . The Bible tells a story of humankind gone astray, taking the entire creation with it, and of God setting out to rescue his creation from its wayward and destructive course. Abraham and his descendants, Israel, become the particular agent of God's rescue operation. . . . Jesus brings this dramatic rescue operation to its climax and conclusion. Much of the NT is an explication of the significance of the cross and resurrection in this grand rescue, and how a rescued people can live as those who will one day inherit and inhabit a rescued creation. (*Dictionary of Biblical Imagery*, ed. Leland Ryken et al. [Downers Grove, IL: IVP Academic, 1998], 705-6, 708-9)

Questions 1-4. Paul prays that the Colossian Christians would be filled with knowledge of God's will so they might live a moral life worthy of the Lord and please him by (1) bearing fruit, (2) growing in knowledge of God, (3) being strengthened in endurance and patience, and (4) giving thanks to the Father. God does not reveal this through secret wisdom but through the person and work of Jesus Christ.

Question 6. It is important for us to understand our previous status before God ("aliens" and "enemies") in contrast to our status after coming to faith in Jesus Christ ("holy," "without blemish," and "free from accusation"). Not only has our status changed 180 degrees in the Savior, but also our lives have become new in Christ as Lord and we begin to live in the Spirit.

Question 7. Here Paul is arguing against what Dietrich Bonhoeffer termed "cheap grace" or what others have called "easy believism." Bonhoeffer said,

> Cheap grace is the preaching of forgiveness without requiring repentance, baptism without church discipline, Communion without confession, absolution without personal confession. Cheap grace is grace without discipleship, grace without the cross, grace without Jesus Christ, living and incarnate. (Dietrich Bonhoeffer, *The Cost of Discipleship* [New York: Touchstone, 1959], 44-45)

Regarding easy believism, Billy Graham said, "People believe easily in a God who makes no demands, but this is not the God of the Bible. . . . [They think] they can believe in Jesus Christ without being changed" (Billy Graham, "An Interview with Billy Graham," *EFCA* [blog], November 8, 2013, www.efca.org/blog/understanding-scripture/interview-billy-graham).

Question 8. *Hope* is not something good we wish to come true but have no basis for believing it will. Here Paul is speaking of something we expect with confidence—something we look forward to and know it will happen.

STUDY 6. RECONCILERS. PHILEMON 1-25

PURPOSE: To understand that since we have been reconciled to God through Jesus Christ, we should actively seek to be ministers of reconciliation.

Question 1. Paul is literally a prisoner in chains (vv. 1, 9, 13), most likely in Rome. Timothy, who accompanied Paul on some of his missionary journeys, is now with Paul. In verse 23 we see that Epaphras is a fellow prisoner with Paul. And Paul is also accompanied by Mark, Aristarchus, Demas, and Luke (v. 24), who appear to be free. The letter is written to Philemon and to the church that meets in Philemon's home, probably in Colossae, which means that Philemon is most likely a wealthy man of high status.

Question 3. Philemon has "refreshed the hearts of the Lord's people" (v. 7). Undoubtedly Paul is referring to spiritual refreshment but also physical and material refreshment. Wealthy patrons of a church often held meals in their homes for others and would even host travelers in their homes.

Question 4. Onesimus is Philemon's runaway slave who has ended up in Paul's company. If he wasn't already, Onesimus now is a follower of Christ, and he has been helpful to Paul. In Greek the name Onesimus means "helpful" or "beneficial." Paul plays off his name to say that this young man now in Christ is not only a new person but he has been beneficial to the apostle and will be so when he returns to Philemon.

Question 5. Paul is not only implying that Philemon should spare Onesimus's life (according to Roman law Philemon could legally execute Onesimus) but accept him as "no longer a slave" but as a "dear brother." Philemon should welcome Onesimus as if he were welcoming Paul himself.

Question 7. Paul appeals to Philemon on the basis of love (v. 9). Onesimus is Paul's "very heart" (v. 12). Paul does not want to force a decision of Philemon (v. 14). Paul will pay Philemon for anything Onesimus might have stolen or for the work lost on account of Onesimus's departure (v. 18). However, Paul reminds Philemon that Philemon owes his "very self" to Paul (v. 19). Paul then appeals to Philemon's Christian character: "refresh my heart in Christ," be "obedient," "do even more than I ask" (vv. 20-21).

STUDY 7. RUNNERS. HEBREWS 12:1-13

PURPOSE: To observe the Lord's example and refocus our discipline as we run the spiritual race set before us by the pioneer and perfecter of our faith.

Question 1. The *Dictionary of Biblical Imagery* notes:

> The unknown author of Hebrews references the race imagery of the Greek and Roman sports world and athletes' self-control and perseverance, running for a reward or goal of faith completed, a prize that is imperishable and eternal, unlike the winner's award at the Isthmian games: "a celery crown." (*Dictionary of Biblical Imagery*, 693)

Question 3. Ancient runners ran without clothes because clothes would hinder them or even entangle them. Likewise, we should get rid of ("throw off") any beliefs, attitudes, habits, or behaviors that might interfere with or even halt our progress in our Christian life.

Questions 4-5. We runners should look to Jesus as our example and inspiration. He is the "pioneer" or leader in the race of faith; he sets our pace. Jesus is also faith's *perfecter*. He has realized faith to the fullest from start to finish and has fulfilled God's promises for all who believe. He has endured far more than we have (opposition from sinners, scorn, the cross, shame) for "the joy set before him" (v. 2). When we keep our eyes on our Pacesetter, we will "not grow weary and lose heart" (v. 3).

Question 6. It takes great discipline to become a successful athlete. Even the most accomplished professional athletes depend on the guidance of their coach, who "disciplines" them. If we are going to "run with perseverance the race" (v. 1), we need to be taught (discipled/coached) by the Lord, the pioneer and perfecter of faith.

STUDY 8. WORSHIPERS. REVELATION 5:1-14; 19:1-8

PURPOSE: To realize that we must praise and worship only the risen, reigning Lamb of God, Jesus the Christ.

Note. The vision of Revelation, with its myriad symbols and signs, can overwhelm readers, causing some to give up reading it. However, we must remember it was given by the Spirit *for Christians*. So, with the Spirit's help, we can understand and learn from it. "Instead of trying to decode every part of the throne of God, try to imagine what can be seen and heard. . . . Worship is not an action but a reaction, a response evoked by a vision of God's glory" (*NIV Quiet Time Bible* [Downers Grove, IL: InterVarsity Press, 1996], 427).

Question 3. The Lion of Judah is a reference to Jesus, who was of the tribe of Judah. The patriarch Judah was associated with the royal lion in Genesis 49:9-10. And lions were viewed by ancient people, as they are today, as the king of the beasts.

Question 4. In this passage we run into some of the strange imagery of the book of Revelation. Try not to get bogged down in this imagery. Regarding the Lamb's seven horns and seven eyes, scholar Craig Keener says:

> The imagery of horns as symbols for authority is rooted in Daniel 8. The seven eyes ranging throughout the earth are from Zechariah 3:9 and 4:10. John might understand them as referring to angels (the image in Zechariah is modeled after Persian royal emissaries) in Zechariah 1:10 and 6:5-7, or to God's Spirit in Zechariah 4:6. At any rate, the eyes in Zechariah are God's eyes; here they belong to the Lord Jesus. (Craig Keener, *Bible Background Commentary: New Testament* [Downers Grove, IL: IVP Academic, 2014], 740)

Question 5. The four groups who worship the Lamb are (1) the four living creatures, (2) the twenty-four elders, (3) thousands of angels, and (4) every creature in heaven and on earth and under the earth. Regarding the four living creatures, these are cherubim (special angels) found in the Old Testament book of Ezekiel (see chaps. 1 and 10). The twenty-four elders have variously been interpreted as Old Testament orders of priests, the number of books in the Old Testament canon, or the twelve tribes of Israel plus the twelve apostles.

Question 7. In Revelation 18, the great whore Babylon, who stands opposed to God, has fallen, so there is rejoicing in heaven. Now, in contrast to the funeral-like feeling of chapter 18, in chapter 19 heaven is preparing for the great banquet following the "wedding of the Lamb" (v. 7). Again, Keener explains,

> In Isaiah 25:6-7 God announces a great banquet for all peoples (cf. Rev 19:7), and in Isaiah 25:8 God's people celebrate their salvation, declaring, "let us rejoice and be glad" in the salvation God had enacted on their behalf. . . . The Old Testament and later Jewish literature often compared Israel to a bride wedded to God; cf. Revelation 21:2. The messianic age or world to come was also often portrayed as a banquet. (Keener, *Bible Background Commentary*, 768)

Bill Weimer, a retired Navy chaplain of twenty-six years, is pastor emeritus of Mariner Sands Chapel, an ecumenical congregation in Stuart, Florida. In the 1960s he became an active Christian through InterVarsity Christian Fellowship, and his wife, Eathel (Bowie), was one of the first female InterVarsity staff workers in the South. For more than five decades they have led Bible discussions on college campuses, at military commands, and for six congregations. They now live in Atlantic Beach, Florida, where they lead various Scripture studies.

WHAT SHOULD WE STUDY NEXT?

LifeGuide® BIBLE STUDIES

A good place to continue your study of Scripture would be with a book study. Many groups begin with a Gospel such as *Mark* (20 studies by Jim Hoover) or *John* (26 studies by Douglas Connelly). These guides are divided into two parts so that if twenty or twenty-six weeks seems like too much to do at once, the group can feel free to do half and take a break with another topic. Later you might want to come back to it. You might prefer to try a shorter letter. *Philippians* (9 studies by Donald Baker), *Ephesians* (11 studies by Andrew T. and Phyllis J. Le Peau), and *1 & 2 Timothy and Titus* (11 studies by Pete Sommer) are good options. If you want to vary your reading with an Old Testament book, consider *Ecclesiastes* (12 studies by Bill and Teresa Syrios) for a challenging and exciting study.

There are a number of interesting topical LifeGuide studies as well. Here are some options for filling three or four quarters of a year:

BASIC DISCIPLESHIP

Christian Beliefs, 12 studies by Stephen Eyre
Christian Character, 12 studies by Andrea Sterk & Peter Scazzero
Christian Disciplines, 12 studies by Andrea Sterk & Peter Scazzero
Evangelism, 12 studies by Rebecca Manley Pippert & Ruth Siemens

BUILDING COMMUNITY

Christian Community, 10 studies by Rob Suggs
Fruit of the Spirit, 9 studies by Hazel Offner
Spiritual Gifts, 8 studies by R. Paul Stevens

CHARACTER STUDIES

New Testament Characters, 10 studies by Carolyn Nystrom
Old Testament Characters, 12 studies by Peter Scazzero
1 & 2 Kings, 10 studies by Carolyn Nystrom
Women of the Old Testament, 12 studies by Gladys Hunt

THE TRINITY

Meeting God, 12 studies by J. I. Packer
Meeting Jesus, 13 studies by Leighton Ford
Meeting the Spirit, 10 studies by Douglas Connelly